The Backpack Activity Book

Buster Books

ILLUSTRATED BY
JOHN BIGWOOD & JOSEPH WILKINS

EDITED BY
HELEN BROWN

DESIGNED BY
JACK CLUCAS

COVER DESIGN BY
ANGIE ALLISON & NANCY LESCHNIKOFF

ADDITIONAL ARTWORK BY
ANDY ROWLAND, CLIVE GOODAYER & DANIEL SANCHEZ LIMON

First published in Great Britain in 2019 by Buster Books, an imprint of
Michael O'Mara Books Limited, 9 Lion Yard, Tremadoc Road, London SW4 7NQ

W www.mombooks.com/buster   f Buster Books   🐦 @BusterBooks

ISBN: 978-1-78055-605-5

3 5 7 9 10 8 6 4 2

This book was printed in December 2019 by
Gutenberg Press Ltd, Gudja Road,
Tarxien GXQ 2902, Malta.

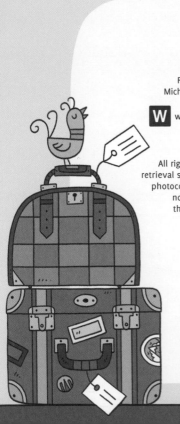

HOW TO USE THIS BOOK

This book is bursting with puzzles to make
any journey fly by. All you need are pens
and pencils to fill your travels with fun.

You can work through the book from
the beginning or dip in and out.

Follow the instructions on each page and,
once a puzzle is completed, check the
answer at the back of the book.

What are you waiting for? Grab your
pens and pencils and get going!

FAIRGROUND FUN

Draw a line from the family to the chair-swing ride as fast as you can without coming off the path. Next, have a go with the opposite hand, and then try it with your eyes closed.

GET PACKING

Circle three items that you would not take on holiday.

HANGING OUT

Guide the sloth down the tree using only the clear branches.
Avoid the tropical animals and leaves that are in the way.

HOW TO DRAW A PELICAN

Follow these steps to draw your own pelican below.

1) Draw a body.

2) Add a beak and tail.

3) Draw a pair of feet.

4) Now add a wing and an eye.

Did you know?
A pelican's pouch is called a gular.

SWEET SUDOKU

Fill in the grid with these six types of ice lollies. Each row, column and six-square block must contain one of each.

Look at the example on the right.

TRAFFIC CONE CONUNDRUM

Can you form each of the totals below by adding together one number from each section of the traffic cone?

5
2
7

6
8
10

1
9
17

TOTALS: 12 = ... + ... + ...

21 = ... + ... + ...

32 = ... + ... + ...

MAGICAL SEARCH

This shop sells unicorn floats but one looks different.
Can you find the odd one out?

FLAGS OF THE WORLD

Write the name of the country that each flag belongs to in the spaces below. The first letter has been added to help you get started.

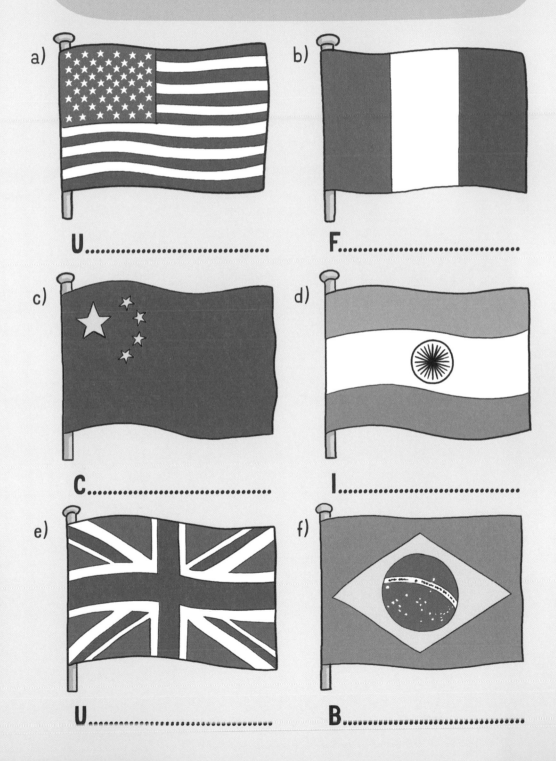

a)

U................................

b)

F................................

c)

C................................

d)

I................................

e)

U................................

f)

B................................

PINEAPPLE CHALLENGE

Draw pineapples on the leafy plants so that the pineapples on each side of the triangle add up to 15. Each plant must have between one and seven pineapples, and no two plants within a side can have the same amount.

SURF'S UP

Ellen, Fred, Robert, Luna and Ben took part in a surfing competition. Ellen finished before Fred but closely behind Luna. Robert finished behind Fred but before Ben. Can you work out which position each surfer finished in? Write each name under the correct award below.

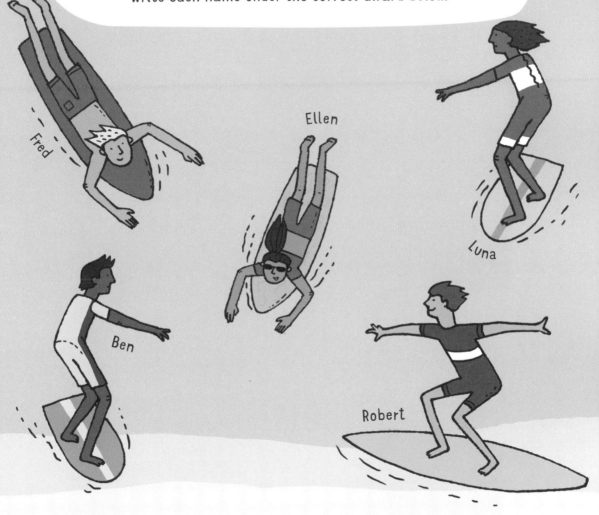

WHEELY FUN MATCH UP

Draw a line to match each bike to its twin.

FIND THE CAPITAL CITY

Can you solve this capital cities wordsearch?

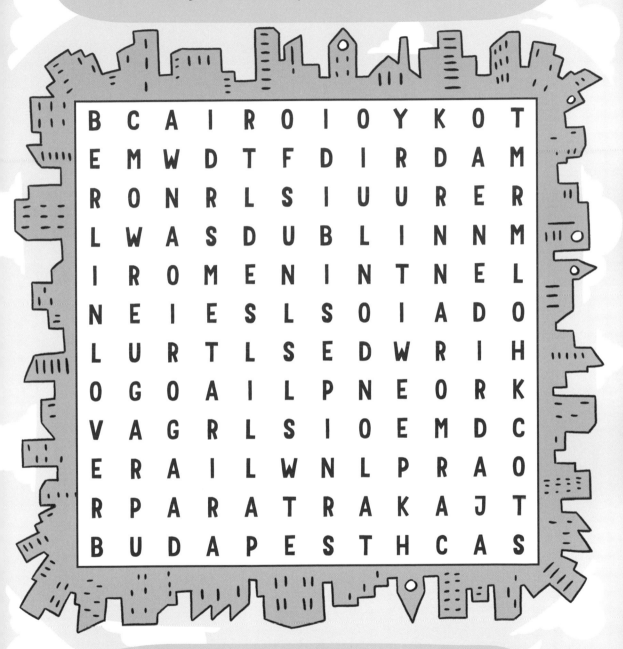

```
B C A I R O I O Y K O T
E M W D T F D I R D A M
R O N R L S I U U R E R
L W A S D U B L I N N M
I R O M E N I N T N E L
N E I E S L S O I A D O
L U R T L S E D W R I H
O G O A I L P N E O R K
V A G R L S I O E M D C
E R A I L W N L P R A O
R P A R A T R A K A J T
B U D A P E S T H C A S
```

Berlin   Jakarta   Prague
Budapest   London   Rome
Cairo   Madrid   Stockholm
Dublin   Paris   Tokyo

HOTEL CAROUSEL

Direct the bags along the correct path in the hotel reception to reach the people waiting for them at the front desk.

FRONT DESK

MAP MAYHEM

You're visiting a theme park. Can you find all of the rides?
Work out the coordinates for each ride listed below.

1. Ferris wheel .... 2. Rollercoaster .... 3. Swinging chairs ....

4. Banana ride .... 5. Spinning teacups ....

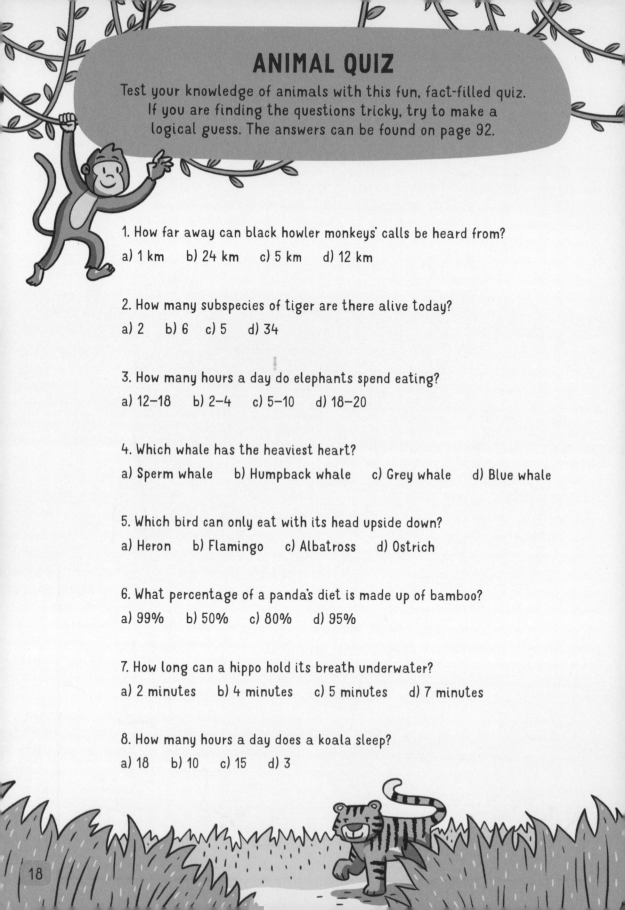

ANIMAL QUIZ

Test your knowledge of animals with this fun, fact-filled quiz.
If you are finding the questions tricky, try to make a
logical guess. The answers can be found on page 92.

1. How far away can black howler monkeys' calls be heard from?
a) 1 km   b) 24 km   c) 5 km   d) 12 km

2. How many subspecies of tiger are there alive today?
a) 2   b) 6   c) 5   d) 34

3. How many hours a day do elephants spend eating?
a) 12–18   b) 2–4   c) 5–10   d) 18–20

4. Which whale has the heaviest heart?
a) Sperm whale   b) Humpback whale   c) Grey whale   d) Blue whale

5. Which bird can only eat with its head upside down?
a) Heron   b) Flamingo   c) Albatross   d) Ostrich

6. What percentage of a panda's diet is made up of bamboo?
a) 99%   b) 50%   c) 80%   d) 95%

7. How long can a hippo hold its breath underwater?
a) 2 minutes   b) 4 minutes   c) 5 minutes   d) 7 minutes

8. How many hours a day does a koala sleep?
a) 18   b) 10   c) 15   d) 3

DOT-TO-DOT

Join the dots to discover a woodland creature hiding in
the trees, then colour in the scene to bring it to life.

MASTER BUILDER

This is a picture of the Eiffel Tower in Paris, France.
Using the squares in the grid below, can you copy it?

ANIMAL EYE SPY

Your challenge is to spot all the creatures shown below when you're out and about. Cross each one off once you've seen it.

FERRY LOADING

Add up the weight of the luggage in each line and work out which line of cars is carrying the lightest load.

3 kg
7 kg
12 kg
11 kg
9 kg
8 kg
2 kg

Line 1

15 kg
10 kg
5 kg
3 kg
8 kg
13 kg

Line 2

13 kg
20 kg
9 kg
12 kg
8 kg

Line 3

22

SPOT THE DIFFERENCE

Can you find the six differences between these two tropical snapshots?

WHAT'S THE TIME?

Read the description below and draw a line from each person to their watch. The first one has been done for you.

Ruby is on a work trip in London. The time in London is 10:00am.
Kenneth has arrived in Russia which is 2 hours ahead of London.
Joseph is on the way to Egypt which is 1 hour behind Russia.
Alfie is on holiday in New York which is 6 hours behind Egypt.
Lauren is travelling to Thailand which is 11 hours ahead of New York.
Raj has been to Australia which is 4 hours ahead of Thailand.

11:00   5:00   20:00   10:00   16:00   12:00

Raj   Ruby   Joseph   Lauren   Kenneth   Alfie

FLAMINGO FEAT

Guide the flamingos to the water using the stepping stones. Draw a line from the Mummy flamingo to the water by stepping on answers that are multiples of 6. Draw a line from the baby chicks by stepping on answers that are multiples of 4.

WATER WORLD MAZE

Which swimmer will come out of which flume?

SWIMMER 1 ....   SWIMMER 2 ....   SWIMMER 3 ....   SWIMMER 4 ....

TRUE OR FALSE?

Read the eight statements below. Write a 'T' in the box if you think it's true, or an 'F' in the box if you think it's false. The answers can be found on page 92.

1. Botanists study plants.

2. There are two different types of rainforests.

3. A quarter of natural medicines have been discovered in rainforests.

4. The tiger is the smallest species of the cat family.

5. Rainforests are found on every continent on Earth.

6. Most beetles only live for a year.

7. Butterflies are not actually insects.

8. Snakes do not have eyelids.

MAGIC MIRROR CHALLENGE

Can you choose the correct mirror image reflection for each picture?

	1	2	3

a

b

c

28

CODE BREAKER

The picture below can be unscrambled to reveal a monument.
Can you name the landmark and where it is located?
Write the answers in the space below.

ANTARCTICA ART

Draw spots on 20% of the 20 emperor penguins.
Draw stripes on 25% of the emperor penguins left blank.
Draw swirls on 75% of the remaining blank emperor penguins.

How many emperor penguins are left blank?

COUNTRY CROSSWORD

Can you crack this country-themed crossword?

ACROSS
3. World's largest country by area (6)
4. Paris is the capital city (6)
7. Connected to Sweden by a bridge (7)
8. Sometimes known as an 'island continent' (9)

DOWN
1. Ancient theatre originated here (6)
2. First tropical country to send a bobsleigh team to the Winter Olympics (7)
5. New Delhi is the capital city (5)
6. Largest population in the world live here (5)

EVEN AND ODD STONES

Help the frogs get to the central lilypad by drawing a line between the stepping stones. Mummy frog can only hop on stepping stones with answers that are even numbers and baby frog can only hop on stones with answers that are odd numbers.

Mummy frog

8x4 =

7+3 =

6-2 =

12-3 =

9-2 =

15+2 =

14+8 =

3-1 =

7x4 =

5x2 =

5x3 =

15-6 =

5+2 =

8-3 =

13-2 =

Baby frog

7+6 =

12+9 =

8+4 =

BEACH DISCOVERY

You have found a rare species of sea turtle at
the beach and the local paper wants to interview you.
Answer the questions below to share the discovery.

DAILY NEWS

How did you find the sea turtle?

What did the sea turtle look like?

What did you do after you found the sea turtle?

Sea turtles are endangered. What can people do to help protect them?

TIME ZONE CONUNDRUM

It's 11:00am in London. Peru is five hours behind, Moscow is three hours ahead and Paris is one hour ahead. Write the name of the country under the clock displaying the correct time.

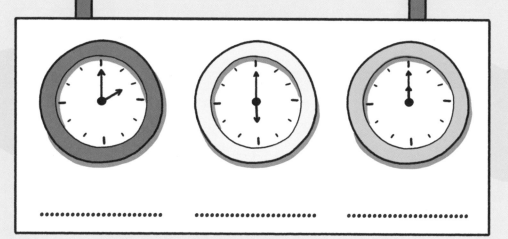

....

HIT THE SLOPES

Draw a line to guide the skier down the slope.
Be careful not to run into any dead ends.

PACKING LIST

Edith and Jaiden are packing for their holiday. They are travelling around the world so are visiting lots of different countries. The items that they will need each day are displayed below.

How many boarding passes will they need for a trip lasting three days? ....

How many train tickets will they need for a holiday lasting two weeks? ....

How many books will they need for a holiday lasting three weeks? ....

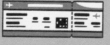

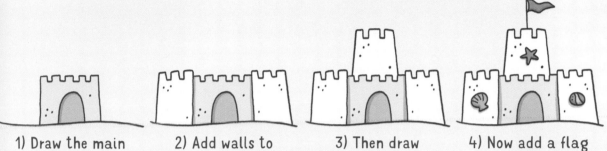

HOW TO DRAW A SANDCASTLE
Follow these steps to draw your own sandcastle below.

1) Draw the main entrance.

2) Add walls to your castle.

3) Then draw a turret.

4) Now add a flag and decoration.

Did you know?
There are over 4,500
species of crabs.

37

TAXI JUMBLE

The vehicles below have been jumbled up.

How many vehicles can you count in this collection?

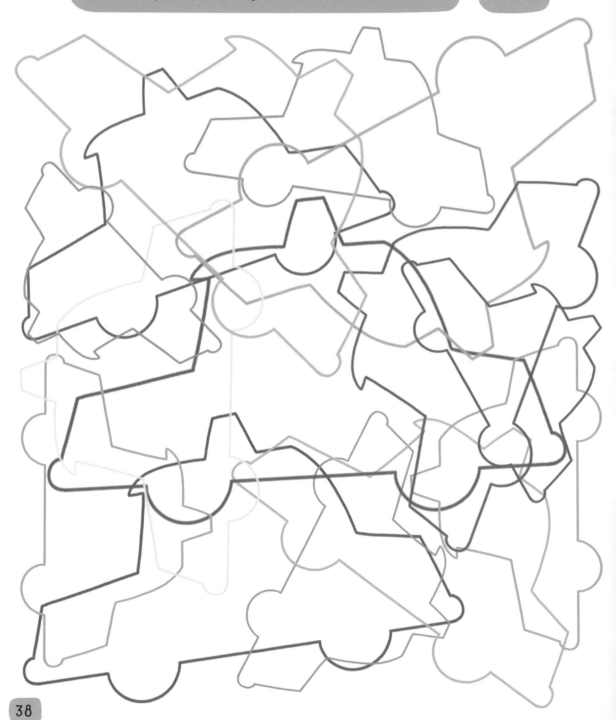

FARMYARD FUN

Can you draw three straight lines to divide the field into four areas? Each area must contain one tree, one sheep and one hay bale.

PAIR THEM UP

Draw lines to connect each pair of identical objects together. The lines must not cross or touch each other, and only one line is allowed in each grid square. You are not allowed to use diagonal lines.

Look at the example on the right.

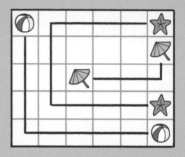

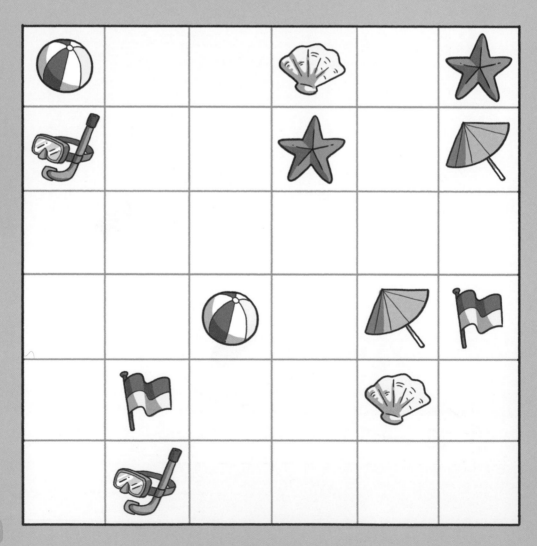

ORIGAMI OWL

Follow the instructions on the back to fold this page into a woodland owl.

 Cut along the outside line.

Step 1 (yellow): Fold along this dotted line.

Step 2 (red): Fold these corners behind.

Step 3 (purple): Turn over and fold corner tips up.

Step 4 (blue): Fold bottom corners in to stand your owl upright.

42

LUGGAGE MIX UP

The piece of luggage that belongs to you has a tag,
red straps and a yellow sticker. Can you find your bag?

TENT SUDOKU

Fill in the grid with these six types of tent. Each row, column and six-square block must contain one of each.

Look at the example on the right.

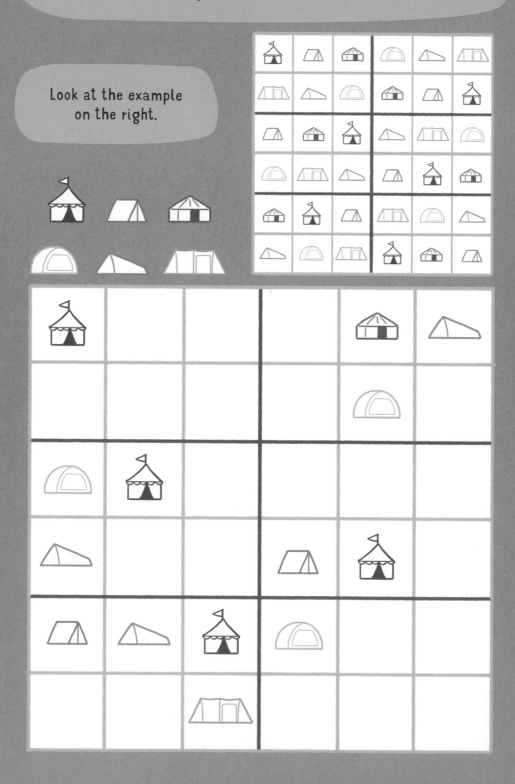

JIGSAW JUMBLE

Can you work out what this picture would be if
all the jigsaw pieces were fitted together?

DESERT TREK

Draw a line to lead the camel through the desert to the water.

PACKING JUMBLE

The airport essentials below have been jumbled up.

How many separate items can you count in this collection?

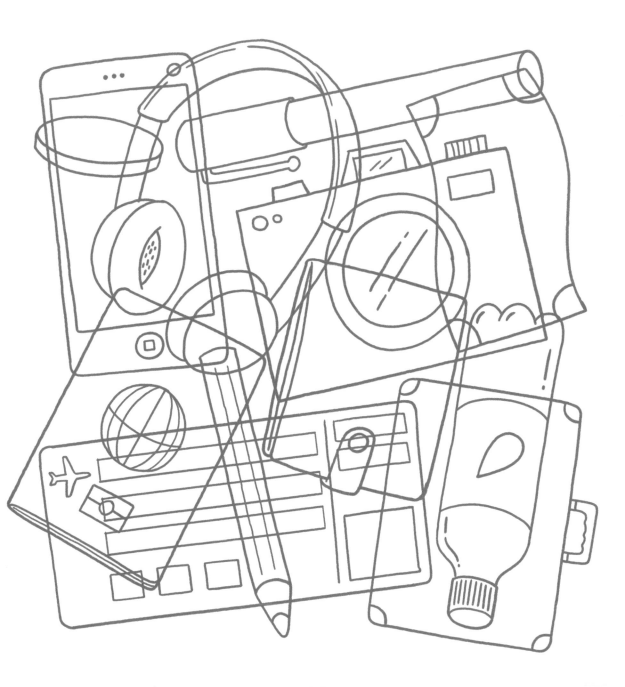

WILDLIFE WATCH

Reach the exit by guiding the jeep through the safari park.

EXIT

BUG WATCH

Circle the insects that have a matching pair.

How many insects do not have a pair?

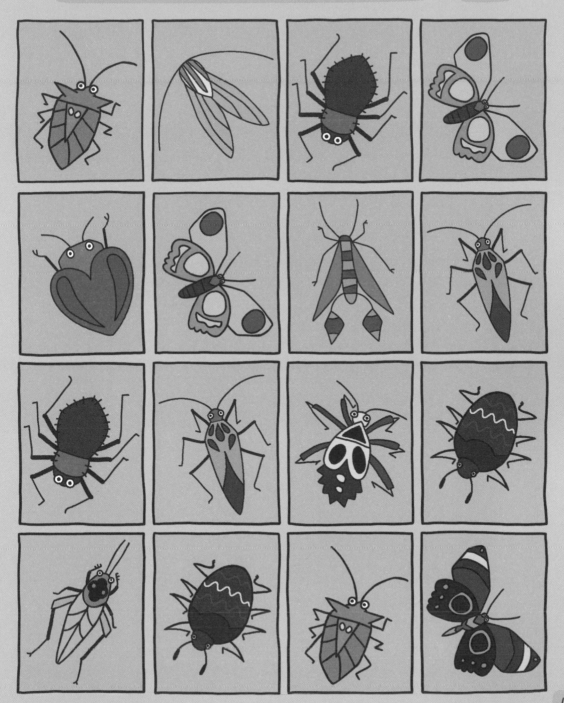

CAMPER VAN DASH

Draw a line from the camper van to the cabin as fast as you can without driving off the road. Next, have a go with the opposite hand, and then try it with your eyes closed.

CABIN

TOWN

TRANSPORT EYE SPY

Your challenge is to spot all the transport
items shown below when you're out and about.
Cross each one off once you've seen it.

  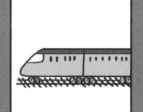 

DOT-TO-DOT

Connect the dots to take a voyage under the sea,
then colour the scene in to bring it to life.

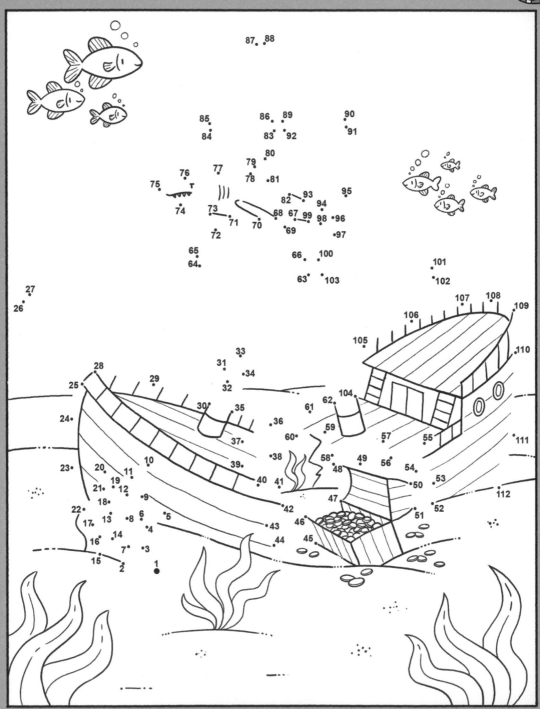

MEMORY SQUARES

Study this page for one minute. Try to remember which pictures are in which squares. Then turn to page 54 and see if you can fill in the blanks correctly.

MEMORY SQUARES

Turn to page 53 to find out how to play this game.

WILD WALKER

Draw a line from the explorer to the tent as fast as you can without coming off the path. Next, have a go with the opposite hand, and then try it with your eyes closed.

55

OCEAN QUIZ

Test your knowledge of the ocean with this fun, fact-filled quiz. If you are finding the questions tricky, try to make a logical guess. The answers can be found on page 94.

1. Approximately, what percentage of Earth's surface is taken up by oceans?
a) 90%   b) 70%   c) 50%   d) 10%

2. What percentage of Earth's oceans have been explored?
a) 5%   b) 20%   c) 45%   d) 85%

3. What is the deepest known area of Earth's oceans?
a) Mariana Trench   b) Tonga Trench   c) Puerto Rico Trench   d) Philippine Trench

4. Approximately, what percentage of Earth's oxygen is produced by the oceans?
a) 95%   b) 3%   c) 70%   d) 35%

5. Which is the largest ocean in the world?
a) Pacific   b) Arctic   c) Indian   d) Atlantic

6. Which ocean is the Bermuda Triangle located in?
a) Pacific   b) Arctic   c) Indian   d) Atlantic

7. Which ocean is frozen for most of the year?
a) Pacific   b) Arctic   c) Indian   d) Atlantic

8. The 'Ring of Fire' is a string of volcanoes in and around what ocean?
a) Pacific   b) Arctic   c) Indian   d) Southern

CONQUER THE CLIMB

Guide the climber up the rock to reach the top.

GLOBE CONFUSION

One of these keyrings looks different.
Can you find the odd one out?

MASTER BUILDER

This is a picture of the Pyramids in Giza, Egypt.
Using the squares in the grid below, can you copy it?

SURFBOARD DESIGN

Draw stripes on 50% of the surfboards.
Draw circles on 20% of the surfboards left blank.
Draw swirls on 75% of the remaining blank surfboards.

How many surfboards are left blank?

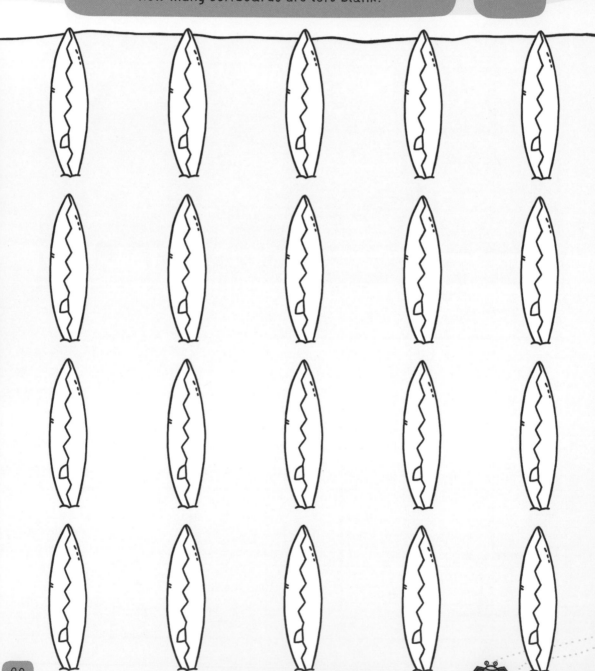

SPOT THE DIFFERENCE

Can you find the six differences
between these two airport scenes?

HELICOPTER PARTS

Circle the group of parts that make up the helicopter below.

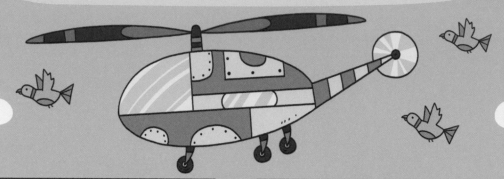

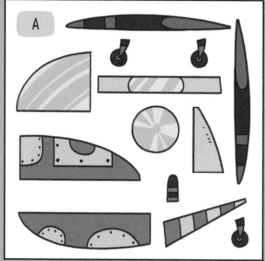

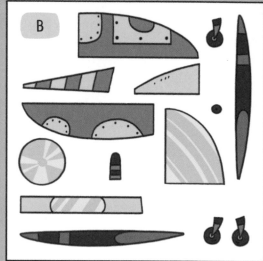

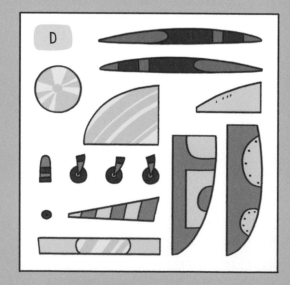

OCEAN JUMBLE

The ocean items below have been jumbled up.

How many items can you count in this collection?

WHICH WAY?

This shop sells compasses, but three are different.
Can you find the three odd ones out?

TRAIN SILHOUETTES

Write each train's number beneath
the silhouette that matches it.

     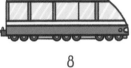

1
2
3
4

  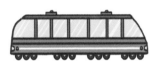   

5
6
7
8

9
10
11
12

A...........
B...........
C...........
D...........

E...........
F...........
G...........
H...........

I...........
J...........
K...........
L...........

65

ANIMAL MATCH UP

The local zoo has a school visit and everyone wants to see a different animal. Read the descriptions below and write the name next to the animal that each child would like to see.

Fred is keen to see a large semi-aquatic mammal.

Frances would like to touch an insect with a unique life cycle.

Mohammed wants to see a cute animal that eats eucalyptus leaves.

Harry is desperate to meet a long reptile that slides along the ground and makes a hissing sound.

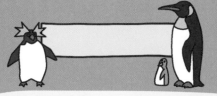

Olivia is hoping to see a mammal that hops around and carries its babies in its pouch.

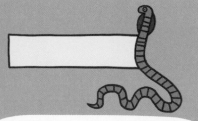

Rodrigo wants to meet a small reptile that has the ability to change colour.

Joanna would like to see an aquatic bird that is usually found in the Southern Hemisphere. It has wings like flippers although it cannot fly.

WILDLIFE ESCAPE

Help the wildlife photographer ride through
the swamp to reach the other side.

EXCHANGE RATE

You are converting your currency (TAN) to the local currency (POL). Look at the exchange rate and work out how much you will receive from the bank.

0.5 TAN
.... POL

2 TAN
.... POL

5 TAN
.... POL

30 TAN
.... POL

3 TAN
.... POL

50 TAN
.... POL

40 TAN
.... POL

35 TAN
.... POL

EXCHANGE RATE
1 TAN = 3 POL

WORLD QUIZ

Test your knowledge of the world with this fun, fact-filled quiz. If you are finding the questions tricky, try to make a logical guess. The answers can be found on page 95.

1. What is the name of Earth's largest hot desert?

a) Arabian   b) Gibson   c) Mojave   d) Sahara

2. At any given time, approximately what percentage of Earth's surface is covered by clouds?

a) 20%   b) 10%   c) 70%   d) 95%

3. What state is the Grand Canyon located in?

a) Alabama   b) Alaska   c) Arkansas   d) Arizona

4. What percentage of Earth's land surface is rainforest?

a) 44%   b) 10%   c) 16%   d) 6%

5. Which country has the largest number of different spoken languages?

a) Papua New Guinea   b) India   c) USA   d) Nigeria

6. Which city has the most skyscrapers?

a) New York City   b) Hong Kong   c) Tokyo   d) Dubai

7. What is the lowest country in the world?

a) Jamaica   b) Belize   c) Maldives   d) Greece

8. How many countries does the Nile River flow through?

a) 1   b) 11   c) 3   d) 9

TREASURE HUNT

Follow the directions below and draw a line to find the buried treasure. Mark the spot with an 'X'.

Start here

Sail west, then head south. Stop when you start to smell smoke. Turn east and sail clockwise around the rocks. Then head south. Search for treasure where the bones meet.

Palm Island

Volcano Mania

Rocky Mountain

Skull Cave

SQUARE TILES

Reach the finish by stepping only on the red, blue and green squares. You can move up, down or across, but not diagonally.

START

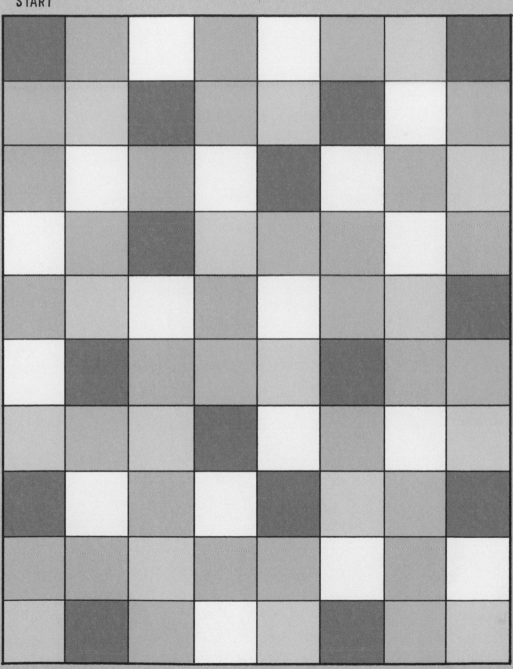

FINISH

HELICOPTER LANDING

Draw a line from the helicopter to the landing pad as fast as you can without coming off the path. Next, have a go with the opposite hand, and then try it with your eyes closed.

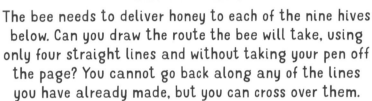

HONEY TRAIL

The bee needs to deliver honey to each of the nine hives below. Can you draw the route the bee will take, using only four straight lines and without taking your pen off the page? You cannot go back along any of the lines you have already made, but you can cross over them.

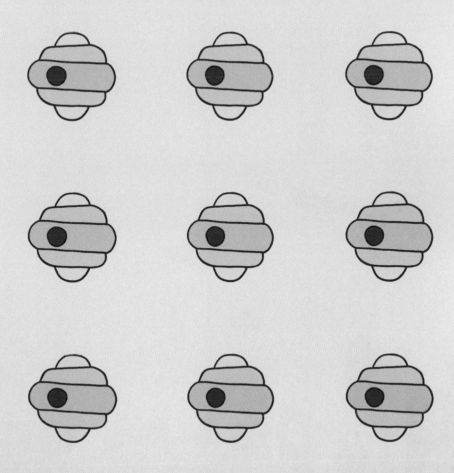

COLD PACKING

Colour the items that you would pack
for a holiday in the Arctic Circle.

MARKET TRADE

Can you calculate how much it would cost
to buy each of the following items?

1. A rug and the fish

2. Two boxes of sweets

3. Two golden trays and the oil lamp

4. Three evil eye necklaces

5. Four green lanterns

£3.00
10% off

£1.50

£2.20

£5.50

£8.25

£6.00
25% off

£15.00
50% off

HOW TO DRAW A TRAIN

Follow these steps to draw your own train below.

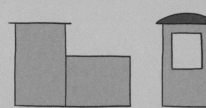 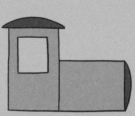  

1) Draw the body of the train.

2) Draw a window, roof and front.

3) Draw the wheels and chimney.

4) Now add the final details.

Did you know? The first steam train was built in 1804.

LUXURY HOTEL

You have been asked to review
your local hotel and spa for the paper.
Answer the questions below to share your review.

DAILY NEWS

Where was the hotel and spa?

How was the food?

What was the best and/or worst spa treatment?

Would you recommend the hotel and spa to a friend?

CODE BREAKER

The picture below can be unravelled to uncover a monument.
Can you name the monument, and where it is located?
Write the answers in the space below.

MOUNTAIN MAZE

Find the way down the mountain to the finish line,
avoiding the broken bridges, puddles and dead ends.

FINISH

HIDDEN PICTURE

Shade in the shapes below by using
the colour of the dot as a guide.

What is the name of the monument
shown, and where would you find it?

....

BAGGAGE STACK

The weight of each bag is the sum of the two bags it's resting on. Fill in the missing weights.

TRAVEL QUIZ

Test your knowledge of travel with this fun, fact-filled quiz.
If you are finding the questions tricky, try to make a logical
guess. The answers can be found on page 96.

1. When was the first hot-air balloon invented?

a) 1760   b) 1783   c) 1812   d) 1894

2. What was the first Apollo mission to get to space?

a) Apollo 2   b) Apollo 7   c) Apollo 6   d) Apollo 9

3. What was the world's fastest plane commonly known as?

a) Songbird   b) Sparrow   c) Blackbird   d) Robin

4. How many horses did it take to carry the Titanic's main anchor?

a) 5   b) 10   c) 50   d) 20

5. Who were the first group of people to build long distance roads?

a) The Romans   b) The Mongols   c) The Ancient Egyptians   d) The Babylonians

6. What was the name of the boats the Vikings used?

a) Tallships   b) Shortships   c) Wideships   d) Longships

7. How long did the Wright Flyer's first flight last?

a) 3½ seconds   b) 5 seconds   b) 7½ seconds   d) 12 seconds

8. Who was the first human in space?

a) Alan Shepard   b) Yuri Gagarin   c) Valentina Tereshkova   d) Neil Armstrong

MEMORY SQUARES

Study this page for one minute. Try to remember which pictures are in which squares. Then turn to page 84 and see if you can fill in the blanks correctly.

MEMORY SQUARES

Turn to page 83 to find out how to play this game.

BRIDGES

Complete these puzzles by drawing straight lines to represent bridges between the numbered islands.

THE RULES

Each island must have the same number of bridges leading off it as the letter printed on it.
A = 1 B = 2 C = 3 D = 4

The lines must not be diagonal, and must not cross each other, or cut across an island.

One line represents one bridge.

You must arrange the bridges so that someone could walk from one island to any other, just using the bridges you've drawn.

EXAMPLE

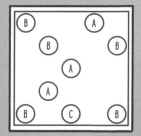

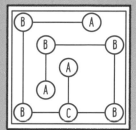

a)
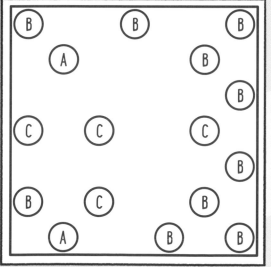

b)
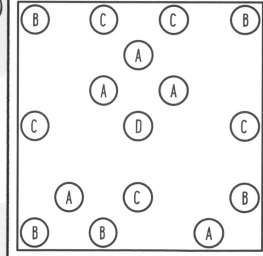

SEASIDE JUMBLE

The seaside objects below have been jumbled up.

How many items can you count in this collection?

PICTURE SUDOKU

Fill in the grid with these six types of surfboards. Each row, column and six-square block must contain one of each.

Look at the example on the right.

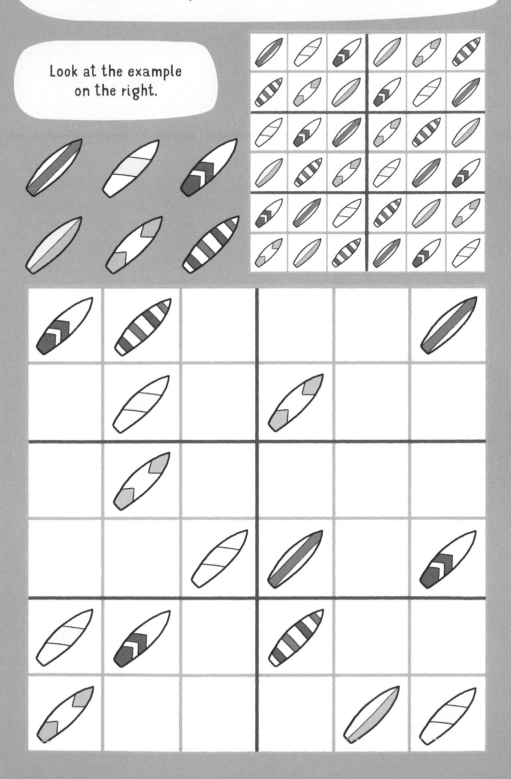

DOTTY POST

Connect the dots to create a postcard. Write a message to a friend, then colour the scene. Don't forget to decorate the stamps.

ODD GIFTS

Can you find the odd one out in each row?

SPOT THE DIFFERENCE

Can you find the six differences between
these two tropical rainforest scenes?

ANSWERS

GET PACKING
Page 5

HANGING OUT
Page 6

SWEET SUDOKU
Page 8

TRAFFIC CONE CONUNDRUM
Page 9
12 = 5 + 6 + 1
21 = 2 + 10 + 9
32 = 7 + 8 + 17

MAGICAL SEARCH
Page 10

FLAGS OF THE WORLD
Page 11
a) United States of America
b) France
c) China
d) India
e) United Kingdom
f) Brazil

SURF'S UP
Page 13
1st - Luna
2nd - Ellen
3rd - Fred
4th - Robert
5th - Ben

WHEELY FUN MATCH UP
Page 14

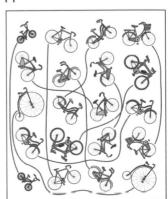

FIND THE CAPITAL CITY
Page 15

HOTEL CAROUSEL
Page 16

MAP MAYHEM
Page 17

1. 2B   3. 5C   5. 3C
2. 6B   4. 3E

ANIMAL QUIZ
Page 18

1. c   3. a   5. b   7. c
2. b   4. d   6. a   8. a

FERRY LOADING
Page 22

Line 1 = 52 kg

SPOT THE DIFFERENCE
Page 23

WHAT'S THE TIME?
Page 24

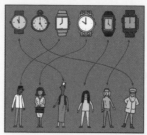

FLAMINGO FEAT
Page 25

WATER WORLD MAZE
Page 26

Swimmer 1 = Flume D
Swimmer 2 = Flume A
Swimmer 3 = Flume B
Swimmer 4 = Flume C

TRUE OR FALSE?
Page 27

1. True   4. False   7. False
2. True   5. False   8. True
3. True   6. True

MAGIC MIRROR CHALLENGE
Page 28

1. b   2. c   3. b

CODE BREAKER
Page 29

Big Ben and the Palace of
Westminster, London, UK

ANTARCTICA ART
Page 30
There are 3 blank emperor penguins.

COUNTRY CROSSWORD
Page 31

EVEN AND ODD STONES
Page 32

TIME ZONE CONUNDRUM
Page 34
In order from left to right:
Moscow, Peru, Paris

HIT THE SLOPES
Page 35

PACKING LIST
Page 36

1. 12   2. 28   3. 21

TAXI JUMBLE
Page 38
There are 14 vehicles.

FARMYARD FUN
Page 39

PAIR THEM UP
Page 40

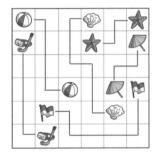

LUGGAGE MIX UP
Page 43

TENT SUDOKU
Page 44

JIGSAW JUMBLE
Page 45
A person kayaking.

DESERT TREK
Page 46

PACKING JUMBLE
Page 47
There are 12 items.

WILDLIFE WATCH
Page 48

BUG WATCH
Page 49
Six insects do not have a pair.

OCEAN QUIZ
Page 56

1. b	3. a	5. a	7. b
2. a	4. c	6. d	8. a

CONQUER THE CLIMB
Page 57

GLOBE CONFUSION
Page 58

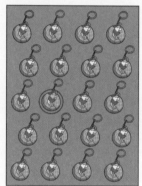

SURFBOARD DESIGN
Page 60
There are 2 blank surfboards.

SPOT THE DIFFERENCE
Page 61

HELICOPTER PARTS
Page 62
Group B

OCEAN JUMBLE
Page 63
There are 7 items.

WHICH WAY?
Page 64

TRAIN SILHOUETTES
Page 65

A3	B9	C6	D11
E2	F10	G4	H12
I1	J5	K8	L7

ANIMAL MATCH UP
Page 66

Chameleon - Rodrigo
Koala - Mohammed
Butterfly - Frances
Penguin - Joanna
Hippo - Fred
Snake - Harry
Kangaroo - Olivia

WILDLIFE ESCAPE
Page 67

EXCHANGE RATE
Page 68
In order from left to right:
1.5 POL, 6 POL
15 POL, 90 POL, 9 POL
150 POL, 120 POL, 105 POL

WORLD QUIZ
Page 69

1. d	3. d	5. a	7. c
2. c	4. d	6. b	8. d

TREASURE HUNT
Page 70
The treasure is under Skull Cave.

SQUARE TILES
Page 71

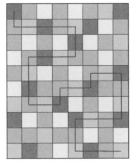

HONEY TRAIL
Page 73

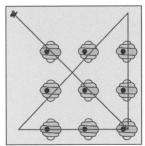

MARKET TRADE
Page 75

1. £9.70	3. £14.50	5. £33
2. £5.40	4. £4.50	

CODE BREAKER
Page 78
Great Pyramid of Giza, Egypt

MOUNTAIN MAZE
Page 79

HIDDEN PICTURE
Page 80
The Statue of Liberty, New York,
United States of America

BAGGAGE STACK
Page 81

TRAVEL QUIZ
Page 82

1. b	3. c	5. a	7. d
2. b	4. d	6. d	8. b

BRIDGES
Page 85

a)

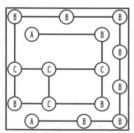

b)

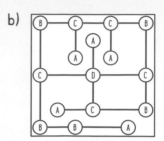

SEASIDE JUMBLE
Page 86
There are 14 items.

PICTURE SUDOKU
Page 87

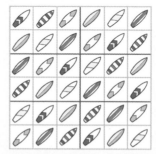

ODD GIFTS
Page 89

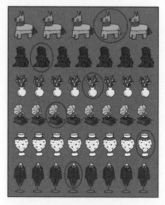

SPOT THE DIFFERENCE
Page 90